TICKET
BOOK

TICKET STUB DIARY

This book belongs to:

Name	
Phone	
Email	

TICKET/EVENT NAME

CITY/PLACE OF EVENT

DATE OF TICKET

START TIME

DURATION

TICKET COST

SUMMARY/TICKET PURCHASE HISTORY

EVENT COMPANION

PASTE TICKET HERE

MY MEMORIES

PASTE PHOTO FROM THE EVENT

TICKET/EVENT NAME

CITY/PLACE OF EVENT

DATE OF TICKET

START TIME

DURATION

TICKET COST

SUMMARY/TICKET PURCHASE HISTORY

EVENT COMPANION

PASTE TICKET HERE

MY MEMORIES

PASTE PHOTO FROM THE EVENT

TICKET/EVENT NAME

CITY/PLACE OF EVENT

DATE OF TICKET

START TIME

DURATION

TICKET COST

SUMMARY/TICKET PURCHASE HISTORY

EVENT COMPANION

PASTE TICKET HERE

MY MEMORIES

PASTE PHOTO FROM THE EVENT

TICKET/EVENT NAME

CITY/PLACE OF EVENT

DATE OF TICKET

START TIME

DURATION

TICKET COST

SUMMARY/TICKET PURCHASE HISTORY

EVENT COMPANION

PASTE TICKET HERE

MY MEMORIES

PASTE PHOTO FROM THE EVENT

TICKET/EVENT NAME

CITY/PLACE OF EVENT

DATE OF TICKET

START TIME

DURATION

TICKET COST

SUMMARY/TICKET PURCHASE HISTORY

EVENT COMPANION

PASTE TICKET HERE

MY MEMORIES

PASTE PHOTO FROM THE EVENT

TICKET/EVENT NAME

CITY/PLACE OF EVENT

DATE OF TICKET

START TIME

DURATION

TICKET COST

SUMMARY/TICKET PURCHASE HISTORY

EVENT COMPANION

PASTE TICKET HERE

MY MEMORIES

PASTE PHOTO FROM THE EVENT

TICKET/EVENT NAME

CITY/PLACE OF EVENT

DATE OF TICKET

START TIME

DURATION

TICKET COST

SUMMARY/TICKET PURCHASE HISTORY

EVENT COMPANION

PASTE TICKET HERE

MY MEMORIES

PASTE PHOTO FROM THE EVENT

TICKET/EVENT NAME

CITY/PLACE OF EVENT

DATE OF TICKET

START TIME

DURATION

TICKET COST

SUMMARY/TICKET PURCHASE HISTORY

EVENT COMPANION

PASTE TICKET HERE

MY MEMORIES

PASTE PHOTO FROM THE EVENT

TICKET/EVENT NAME

CITY/PLACE OF EVENT

DATE OF TICKET

START TIME

DURATION

TICKET COST

SUMMARY/TICKET PURCHASE HISTORY

EVENT COMPANION

PASTE TICKET HERE

MY MEMORIES

PASTE PHOTO FROM THE EVENT

TICKET/EVENT NAME

CITY/PLACE OF EVENT

DATE OF TICKET

START TIME

DURATION

TICKET COST

SUMMARY/TICKET PURCHASE HISTORY

EVENT COMPANION

PASTE TICKET HERE

MY MEMORIES

PASTE PHOTO FROM THE EVENT

TICKET/EVENT NAME

CITY/PLACE OF EVENT

DATE OF TICKET

START TIME

DURATION

TICKET COST

SUMMARY/TICKET PURCHASE HISTORY

EVENT COMPANION

PASTE TICKET HERE

MY MEMORIES

PASTE PHOTO FROM THE EVENT

TICKET/EVENT NAME

CITY/PLACE OF EVENT

DATE OF TICKET

START TIME

DURATION

TICKET COST

SUMMARY/TICKET PURCHASE HISTORY

EVENT COMPANION

PASTE TICKET HERE

MY MEMORIES

PASTE PHOTO FROM THE EVENT

TICKET/EVENT NAME

CITY/PLACE OF EVENT

DATE OF TICKET

START TIME

DURATION

TICKET COST

SUMMARY/TICKET PURCHASE HISTORY

EVENT COMPANION

PASTE TICKET HERE

MY MEMORIES

PASTE PHOTO FROM THE EVENT

TICKET/EVENT NAME

CITY/PLACE OF EVENT

DATE OF TICKET

START TIME

DURATION

TICKET COST

SUMMARY/TICKET PURCHASE HISTORY

EVENT COMPANION

PASTE TICKET HERE

MY MEMORIES

PASTE PHOTO FROM THE EVENT

TICKET/EVENT NAME

CITY/PLACE OF EVENT

DATE OF TICKET

START TIME

DURATION

TICKET COST

SUMMARY/TICKET PURCHASE HISTORY

EVENT COMPANION

PASTE TICKET HERE

MY MEMORIES

PASTE PHOTO FROM THE EVENT

TICKET/EVENT NAME

CITY/PLACE OF EVENT

DATE OF TICKET

START TIME

DURATION

TICKET COST

SUMMARY/TICKET PURCHASE HISTORY

EVENT COMPANION

PASTE TICKET HERE

MY MEMORIES

PASTE PHOTO FROM THE EVENT

TICKET/EVENT NAME

CITY/PLACE OF EVENT

DATE OF TICKET

START TIME

DURATION

TICKET COST

SUMMARY/TICKET PURCHASE HISTORY

EVENT COMPANION

PASTE TICKET HERE

MY MEMORIES

PASTE PHOTO FROM THE EVENT

TICKET/EVENT NAME

CITY/PLACE OF EVENT

DATE OF TICKET

START TIME

DURATION

TICKET COST

SUMMARY/TICKET PURCHASE HISTORY

EVENT COMPANION

PASTE TICKET HERE

MY MEMORIES

PASTE PHOTO FROM THE EVENT

TICKET/EVENT NAME

CITY/PLACE OF EVENT

DATE OF TICKET

START TIME

DURATION

TICKET COST

SUMMARY/TICKET PURCHASE HISTORY

EVENT COMPANION

PASTE TICKET HERE

MY MEMORIES

PASTE PHOTO FROM THE EVENT

TICKET/EVENT NAME

CITY/PLACE OF EVENT

DATE OF TICKET

START TIME

DURATION

TICKET COST

SUMMARY/TICKET PURCHASE HISTORY

EVENT COMPANION

PASTE TICKET HERE

MY MEMORIES

PASTE PHOTO FROM THE EVENT

TICKET/EVENT NAME

CITY/PLACE OF EVENT

DATE OF TICKET

START TIME

DURATION

TICKET COST

SUMMARY/TICKET PURCHASE HISTORY

EVENT COMPANION

PASTE TICKET HERE

MY MEMORIES

PASTE PHOTO FROM THE EVENT

TICKET/EVENT NAME

CITY/PLACE OF EVENT

DATE OF TICKET

START TIME

DURATION

TICKET COST

SUMMARY/TICKET PURCHASE HISTORY

EVENT COMPANION

PASTE TICKET HERE

MY MEMORIES

PASTE PHOTO FROM THE EVENT

TICKET/EVENT NAME

CITY/PLACE OF EVENT

DATE OF TICKET

START TIME

DURATION

TICKET COST

SUMMARY/TICKET PURCHASE HISTORY

EVENT COMPANION

PASTE TICKET HERE

MY MEMORIES

PASTE PHOTO FROM THE EVENT

TICKET/EVENT NAME

CITY/PLACE OF EVENT

DATE OF TICKET

START TIME

DURATION

TICKET COST

SUMMARY/TICKET PURCHASE HISTORY

EVENT COMPANION

PASTE TICKET HERE

MY MEMORIES

PASTE PHOTO FROM THE EVENT

TICKET/EVENT NAME

CITY/PLACE OF EVENT

DATE OF TICKET

START TIME

DURATION

TICKET COST

SUMMARY/TICKET PURCHASE HISTORY

EVENT COMPANION

PASTE TICKET HERE

MY MEMORIES

PASTE PHOTO FROM THE EVENT

TICKET/EVENT NAME

CITY/PLACE OF EVENT

DATE OF TICKET

START TIME

DURATION

TICKET COST

SUMMARY/TICKET PURCHASE HISTORY

EVENT COMPANION

PASTE TICKET HERE

MY MEMORIES

PASTE PHOTO FROM THE EVENT

TICKET/EVENT NAME

CITY/PLACE OF EVENT

DATE OF TICKET

START TIME

DURATION

TICKET COST

SUMMARY/TICKET PURCHASE HISTORY

EVENT COMPANION

PASTE TICKET HERE

MY MEMORIES

PASTE PHOTO FROM THE EVENT

TICKET/EVENT NAME

CITY/PLACE OF EVENT

DATE OF TICKET

START TIME

DURATION

TICKET COST

SUMMARY/TICKET PURCHASE HISTORY

EVENT COMPANION

PASTE TICKET HERE

MY MEMORIES

PASTE PHOTO FROM THE EVENT

TICKET/EVENT NAME

CITY/PLACE OF EVENT

DATE OF TICKET

START TIME

DURATION

TICKET COST

SUMMARY/TICKET PURCHASE HISTORY

EVENT COMPANION

PASTE TICKET HERE

MY MEMORIES

PASTE PHOTO FROM THE EVENT

TICKET/EVENT NAME

CITY/PLACE OF EVENT

DATE OF TICKET

START TIME

DURATION

TICKET COST

SUMMARY/TICKET PURCHASE HISTORY

EVENT COMPANION

PASTE TICKET HERE

MY MEMORIES

PASTE PHOTO FROM THE EVENT

TICKET/EVENT NAME

CITY/PLACE OF EVENT

DATE OF TICKET

START TIME

DURATION

TICKET COST

SUMMARY/TICKET PURCHASE HISTORY

EVENT COMPANION

PASTE TICKET HERE

MY MEMORIES

PASTE PHOTO FROM THE EVENT

TICKET/EVENT NAME

CITY/PLACE OF EVENT

DATE OF TICKET

START TIME

DURATION

TICKET COST

SUMMARY/TICKET PURCHASE HISTORY

EVENT COMPANION

PASTE TICKET HERE

MY MEMORIES

PASTE PHOTO FROM THE EVENT

TICKET/EVENT NAME

CITY/PLACE OF EVENT

DATE OF TICKET

START TIME

DURATION

TICKET COST

SUMMARY/TICKET PURCHASE HISTORY

EVENT COMPANION

PASTE TICKET HERE

MY MEMORIES

PASTE PHOTO FROM THE EVENT

TICKET/EVENT NAME

CITY/PLACE OF EVENT

DATE OF TICKET

START TIME

DURATION

TICKET COST

SUMMARY/TICKET PURCHASE HISTORY

EVENT COMPANION

PASTE TICKET HERE

MY MEMORIES

PASTE PHOTO FROM THE EVENT

TICKET/EVENT NAME

CITY/PLACE OF EVENT

DATE OF TICKET

START TIME

DURATION

TICKET COST

SUMMARY/TICKET PURCHASE HISTORY

EVENT COMPANION

PASTE TICKET HERE

MY MEMORIES

PASTE PHOTO FROM THE EVENT

TICKET/EVENT NAME

CITY/PLACE OF EVENT

DATE OF TICKET

START TIME

DURATION

TICKET COST

SUMMARY/TICKET PURCHASE HISTORY

EVENT COMPANION

PASTE TICKET HERE

MY MEMORIES

PASTE PHOTO FROM THE EVENT

TICKET/EVENT NAME

CITY/PLACE OF EVENT

DATE OF TICKET

START TIME

DURATION

TICKET COST

SUMMARY/TICKET PURCHASE HISTORY

EVENT COMPANION

PASTE TICKET HERE

MY MEMORIES

PASTE PHOTO FROM THE EVENT

TICKET/EVENT NAME

CITY/PLACE OF EVENT

DATE OF TICKET

START TIME

DURATION

TICKET COST

SUMMARY/TICKET PURCHASE HISTORY

EVENT COMPANION

PASTE TICKET HERE

MY MEMORIES

PASTE PHOTO FROM THE EVENT

TICKET/EVENT NAME

CITY/PLACE OF EVENT

DATE OF TICKET

START TIME

DURATION

TICKET COST

SUMMARY/TICKET PURCHASE HISTORY

EVENT COMPANION

PASTE TICKET HERE

MY MEMORIES

PASTE PHOTO FROM THE EVENT

TICKET/EVENT NAME

CITY/PLACE OF EVENT

DATE OF TICKET

START TIME

DURATION

TICKET COST

SUMMARY/TICKET PURCHASE HISTORY

EVENT COMPANION

PASTE TICKET HERE

MY MEMORIES

PASTE PHOTO FROM THE EVENT

TICKET/EVENT NAME

CITY/PLACE OF EVENT

DATE OF TICKET

START TIME

DURATION

TICKET COST

SUMMARY/TICKET PURCHASE HISTORY

EVENT COMPANION

PASTE TICKET HERE

MY MEMORIES

PASTE PHOTO FROM THE EVENT

TICKET/EVENT NAME

CITY/PLACE OF EVENT

DATE OF TICKET

START TIME

DURATION

TICKET COST

SUMMARY/TICKET PURCHASE HISTORY

EVENT COMPANION

PASTE TICKET HERE

MY MEMORIES

PASTE PHOTO FROM THE EVENT

TICKET/EVENT NAME

CITY/PLACE OF EVENT

DATE OF TICKET

START TIME

DURATION

TICKET COST

SUMMARY/TICKET PURCHASE HISTORY

EVENT COMPANION

PASTE TICKET HERE

MY MEMORIES

PASTE PHOTO FROM THE EVENT

TICKET/EVENT NAME

CITY/PLACE OF EVENT

DATE OF TICKET

START TIME

DURATION

TICKET COST

SUMMARY/TICKET PURCHASE HISTORY

EVENT COMPANION

PASTE TICKET HERE

MY MEMORIES

PASTE PHOTO FROM THE EVENT

TICKET/EVENT NAME

CITY/PLACE OF EVENT

DATE OF TICKET

START TIME

DURATION

TICKET COST

SUMMARY/TICKET PURCHASE HISTORY

EVENT COMPANION

PASTE TICKET HERE

MY MEMORIES

PASTE PHOTO FROM THE EVENT

TICKET/EVENT NAME

CITY/PLACE OF EVENT

DATE OF TICKET

START TIME

DURATION

TICKET COST

SUMMARY/TICKET PURCHASE HISTORY

EVENT COMPANION

PASTE TICKET HERE

MY MEMORIES

PASTE PHOTO FROM THE EVENT

TICKET/EVENT NAME

CITY/PLACE OF EVENT

DATE OF TICKET

START TIME

DURATION

TICKET COST

SUMMARY/TICKET PURCHASE HISTORY

EVENT COMPANION

PASTE TICKET HERE

MY MEMORIES

PASTE PHOTO FROM THE EVENT

TICKET/EVENT NAME

CITY/PLACE OF EVENT

DATE OF TICKET

START TIME

DURATION

TICKET COST

SUMMARY/TICKET PURCHASE HISTORY

EVENT COMPANION

PASTE TICKET HERE

MY MEMORIES

PASTE PHOTO FROM THE EVENT

TICKET/EVENT NAME

CITY/PLACE OF EVENT

DATE OF TICKET

START TIME

DURATION

TICKET COST

SUMMARY/TICKET PURCHASE HISTORY

EVENT COMPANION

PASTE TICKET HERE

MY MEMORIES

PASTE PHOTO FROM THE EVENT

TICKET/EVENT NAME

CITY/PLACE OF EVENT

DATE OF TICKET

START TIME

DURATION

TICKET COST

SUMMARY/TICKET PURCHASE HISTORY

EVENT COMPANION

PASTE TICKET HERE

MY MEMORIES

PASTE PHOTO FROM THE EVENT

TICKET/EVENT NAME

CITY/PLACE OF EVENT

DATE OF TICKET

START TIME

DURATION

TICKET COST

SUMMARY/TICKET PURCHASE HISTORY

EVENT COMPANION

PASTE TICKET HERE

MY MEMORIES

PASTE PHOTO FROM THE EVENT

TICKET/EVENT NAME

CITY/PLACE OF EVENT

DATE OF TICKET

START TIME

DURATION

TICKET COST

SUMMARY/TICKET PURCHASE HISTORY

EVENT COMPANION

PASTE TICKET HERE

MY MEMORIES

PASTE PHOTO FROM THE EVENT

TICKET/EVENT NAME

CITY/PLACE OF EVENT

DATE OF TICKET

START TIME

DURATION

TICKET COST

SUMMARY/TICKET PURCHASE HISTORY

EVENT COMPANION

PASTE TICKET HERE

MY MEMORIES

PASTE PHOTO FROM THE EVENT

NOTES

Made in the USA
Las Vegas, NV
28 November 2022

60557013R20061